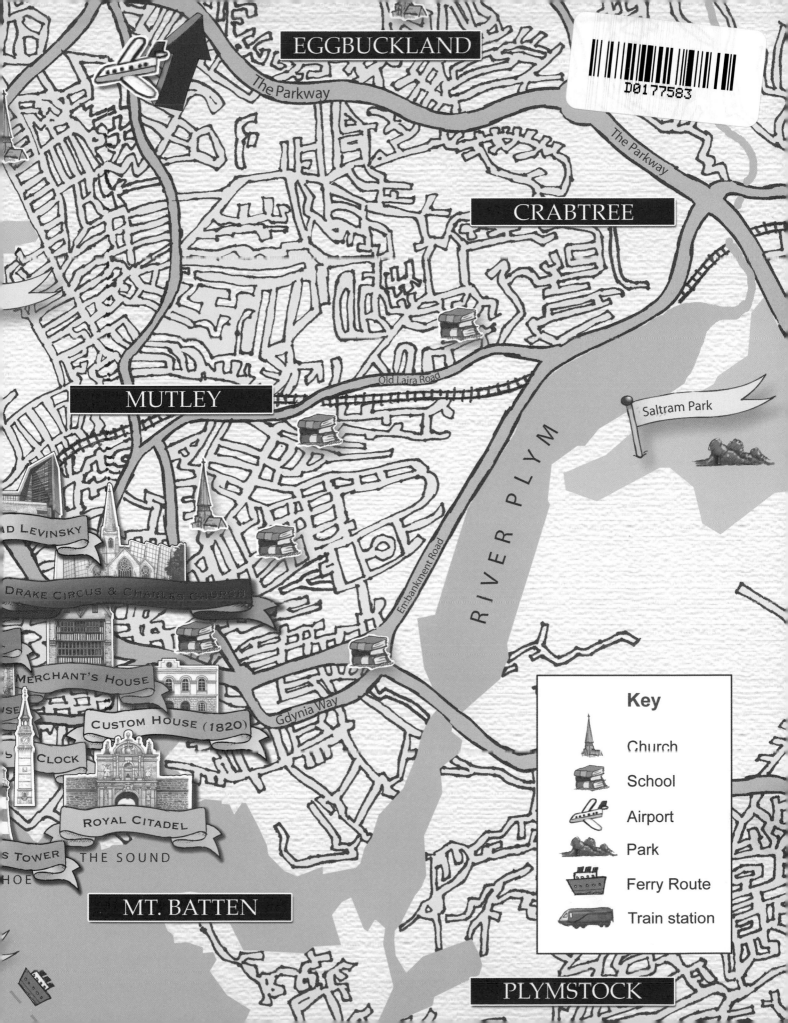

EGGBUCKLAND

The Parkway

The Parkway

CRABTREE

Old Laira Road

Saltram Park

MUTLEY

RIVER PLYM

Embankment Road

D0177583

D LEVINSKY

DRAKE CIRCUS & CHARLES CHURCH

MERCHANT'S HOUSE

CUSTOM HOUSE (1820)

Gdynia Way

Clock

ROYAL CITADEL

S TOWER   THE SOUND

HOE

MT. BATTEN

PLYMSTOCK

Key

Church

School

Airport

Park

Ferry Route

Train station

children's HISTORY of
PLYMOUTH

Writt
Chris P.

HOMETOWN WORLD

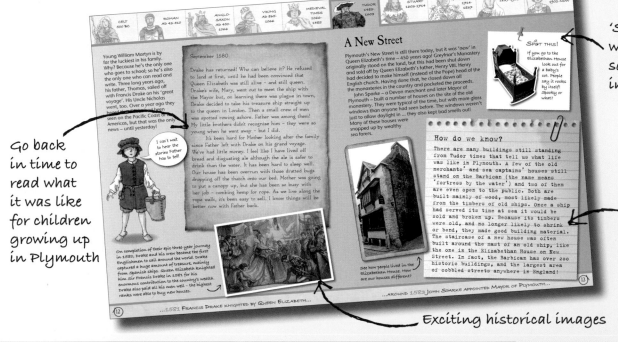

CELT	ROMAN	ANGLO-SAXON

500 BC   400 BC   300 BC   200 BC   100 BC   AD   AD 100   AD 200   AD 300   AD 400   AD 500   AD 600   AD 7...

How well do you know your town?

Have you ever wondered what it would have been like living in Plymouth during Tudor times? Imagine the smells with people throwing food out of windows! What about sailing around the world with Francis Drake and his crew? This book will uncover the important and exciting things that happened in your town.

Want to hear the other good bits? You will love this book! Some rather brainy folk have worked on it to make sure it's fun and informative. So what are you waiting for? Peel back the pages and be amazed at what happened in your town.

Timeline shows which period (dates and people) each spread is talking about

Clear informative text

Hometown facts to amaze you!

Go back in time to read what it was like for children growing up in Plymouth

'Spot this!' game with hints on something to find in your town

Each period in the book ends with a summary explaining how we know about the past

Exciting historical images

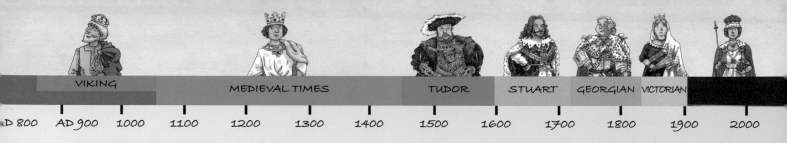

Contents

CELT
500 BC

ROMAN
AD 43-410

ANGLO-
SAXON
AD 450-
1066

VIKING
AD 865-
1066

MEDIEVA[L]
TIMES
1066-
1485

A Trading Port

In the distance but getting bigger by the minute is a large vessel with full sails. Sophia spotted the boat long before the others saw it, when it was still just a tiny speck. Sophia's father, Marcus, is one of the few Romans living in the south-west of England. He is a 'factor', a trader, and the ship belongs to his friend Homer, another factor. Marcus gets ready to receive the ship which is laden with pottery, jewellery, woollen fabrics, sheepskins and furs from the Mediterranean. Marcus also trades live pigs and sheep.

I live at How Stert, which means 'the end of the high ridge'. Today it's called Mount Batten.

Mount Batten

Although the town we now call Plymouth wasn't established until Saxon times, there are signs of nearby settlement that date back much further in history. Some interesting archaeological finds made at Mount Batten over the last 150 years have encouraged experts to believe that Bronze Age people once lived here.

Ancient pieces of jewellery, pottery and metalwork, some of them 3,000 years old, suggest that Mount Batten was an important trading centre for many centuries. People probably lived and worked in the area from 1000 BC right up to the end of the Roman occupation of Britain, in around AD 410.

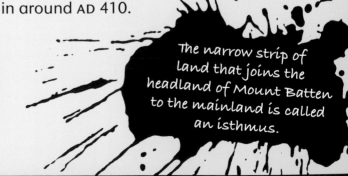

The narrow strip of land that joins the headland of Mount Batten to the mainland is called an isthmus.

Mount Batten as it's seen today.

ABOUT AD 43 ROMANS ARRIVE IN BRITAIN...

TUDOR
1485-1603

STUART
1603-1714

GEORGIAN
1714-1837

VICTORIAN
1837-1901

MODERN
TIMES
1902-NOW

Roman Ships

Mount Batten would have been the perfect location for settlers wanting to protect themselves from attacks coming by land. The settlers would have had a shock when attackers did eventually arrive by sea as they weren't well protected! Most Roman settlements stopped at Exeter so it's more likely that the Romans arrived by boat because the roads were too bad to be used.

Ships like this one would have carried grain and other goods from abroad into the harbour.

SPOT THIS!

Have you seen the plaque by Mount Batten Tower? What does it say?

There's nothing better than having a good dig. You never know what you may find!

How do we know?

The earliest finds recorded at Mount Batten were made in 1832, in the early days of archaeology. Five gold and eight silver coins were found in a crevice in the rocks, followed by further discoveries. They are believed to be pre-Roman.

In the 19th century, the stone from Mount Batten was quarried and used as building material, notably for the Breakwater. In 1864 a Bronze Age cemetery was found at Mount Batten and a Bronze Age mirror was among the treasures unearthed.

Professor Barry Cunliffe, from Oxford University, was in charge of the last major archaeological dig at Mount Batten. He wrote a paper about it, describing the richness and variety of the finds he made there, all of which suggest that this must have been an important trading post for hundreds of years. The local residents were so impressed they named a street in his honour: Cunliffe Avenue.

... ABOUT AD 410 ROMANS LEAVE BRITAIN...

CELT
500 BC

ROMAN
AD 43-410

ANGLO-
SAXON
AD 450-
1066

VIKING
AD 865-
1066

MEDIEVA
TIMES
1066-
1485

Lord of the Manor

The air is heavy with woodsmoke as Saewulf and his cousin, Wulfnoth, follow the plough. They reach into the coarse woollen bags slung across their shoulders and scatter seeds into a deep scar in the rich brown soil. The boy, Snot, Saewulf's son, coaxes the oxen forwards. Black clouds of smoke belch out from the charcoal-making mounds and drift across the tree-lined valley. It will soon be dark, but the field is not yet ploughed. They promised Heca it would be finished by sunset.

Oy! Your food is down the other end!

It was usual for people to share their homes with their livestock. The animals lived at one end of the hut – useful in the winter as they provided extra warmth!

Heca's Bookland

Heca was the Anglo-Saxon lord who held the manor of Eggbuckland, which is north-east of Plymouth today. He gave the area its name, Heca's bookland, which means, 'the land entered in the book as belonging to Heca'. (The book was the Domesday Book.) Anglo-Saxon words were seldom written down, and over many years of mishearing and mispronunciation, the name became Egg Buckland, then just Eggbuckland

There was a settlement by the creek, which housed about ten villagers and eight smallholders — that is eighteen families. Saewulf was a smallholder, which meant that he did not have as much land as a villager. Heca owned a number of manors or villages and he allowed others to work some of his land in return for them helping on his land. A couple of hundred metres above the creek was a tiny, wooden Anglo-Saxon church. Then there was half a hectare of meadowland, 80 hectares of woodland, and farmland roughly a mile and a half long and 400 metres wide.

...AROUND AD 450 ANGLO-SAXONS ARRIVE FROM SCANDINAVIA...

TUDOR
1485-1603

STUART
1603-1714

GEORGIAN
1714-1837

VICTORIAN
1837-1901

MODERN
TIMES
1902-NOW

Anglo Saxon Word

Many of the words we use today come from Anglo-Saxon times. 'Furlong' is made up of two words: furrow and long. It is the typical length of the strip of land Saewulf and others would have farmed. It was important, as it represented the average distance a team of oxen could pull a plough before needing to rest and turn back again. Turning the plough was a tricky manoeuvre for the men and for their oxen.

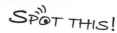

SPOT THIS!

St Edward's Church is thought to be on the same site as the earlier Saxon church. Imagine how important the valley site was.

Most Anglo-Saxons were pagans which meant they worshipped a different god for every area of life.

I'm Ebba, Snot's sister. I'm collecting acorns and birds' eggs to eat.

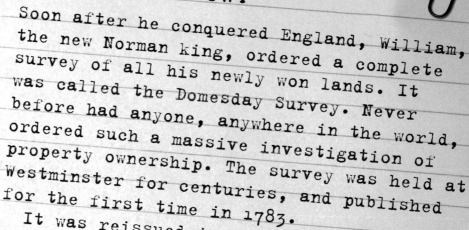

How do we know?

Soon after he conquered England, William, the new Norman king, ordered a complete survey of all his newly won lands. It was called the Domesday Survey. Never before had anyone, anywhere in the world, ordered such a massive investigation of property ownership. The survey was held at Westminster for centuries, and published for the first time in 1783.

It was reissued in 1985, 900 years after it had been started! Now you can find it on the Internet!

From the information gathered in the Domesday Book we can be reasonably sure about how many people lived in 'Buckland' and how big it was. Saewulf, Wulfnoth and Snot were real people who did live there.

CELT
500 BC

ROMAN
AD 43–410

ANGLO-
SAXON
AD 450–
1066

VIKING
AD 865–
1066

MEDIEVAL
TIMES
1066–148

The Priory

There's a new bishop in charge at Plympton Priory – Bishop Warwist. He's a stickler for the rules. He'd only been in his job a couple of weeks when he discovered that some of the monks had families. He was horrified! Monks are supposed to be married only to God! He sent the monks packing, with their families. Some went to work on local farms. The priory owns most of them too. Here's my secret: Father is one of Bishop Warwist's monks! We've gone to live on Uncle Robert's farm. I hope to see Father soon.

I won't miss the food at the priory. It was rather boring!

Plympton had a castle with a 9-metre tower made of stone on the motte.

Plympton was a busy seaport until the River Plym silted up. Trade then moved down the river to Plymouth.

King and Castle

During the end of the Anglo-Saxon period, Plymouth was mainly known as Sutton (meaning the 'south settlement') with just a few scattered farms – most of which were owned by the wealthy Plympton Priory.

Before William the Conqueror came to power in 1066 Plympton had belonged to the Crown. But then William gave the manor of Plympton to one of his relations, Reviers Baldwin. Then, in 1135, one of Baldwin's descendants (also called Baldwin and known as the Earl of Devon) had an argument with King Stephen about some land he had been promised. The argument ended in a battle at Exeter. Baldwin lost the fight, and King Stephen sent about 100 men down to Plympton to batter Baldwin's castle. Luckily, the Earl of Devon survived the attack, and went on to establish a new town: Plympton Erle ('the earl's town') near the castle.

TUDOR
1485-1603

STUART
1603-1714

GEORGIAN
1714-1837

VICTORIAN
1837-1901

MODERN
TIMES
1902-
NOW

Two Plymptons

It was 200 years before another community grew up in sight of the castle, near the old priory. Plympton St Mary was named after the fine medieval church of St Mary. It still stands today, as does Plympton Erle (now known as Plympton St Maurice). You can even see the castle and, though it isn't complete, the views from its wall show how well positioned it was to defend itself from attack. You can find traces of the old priory in some of the houses around St Mary's Church.

Plympton Castle as it's seen today. There is a blue plaque that says the castle was built by the Earls of Devon to defend Plympton manor.

ancient borough · stannary town
1155   1328
Plympton St. Maurice

Plympton St Maurice was a stannary town, which means that tin was assessed for its value here.

SPOT THIS!

This is a gargoyle from St Mary's Church. It gargles or spits rainwater through its open mouth. How many gargoyles can you spot at the church?

How do we know?

It is recorded that, in 1121, Bishop Warwist founded a new priory at Plympton. It is said that the Bishop was unhappy that some members of the old clergy were secretly married, so he decided to enforce stricter discipline and replace the worldly monks with regular religious men. By the time of the Dissolution of the Monasteries in 1539, the priory at Plympton had become rich and powerful.

In 1254, Plymouth (named as being at the mouth of the River Plym and no longer Sutton) was recognised as a town and granted a Royal Charter.

...1254 ROYAL CHARTER GRANTED TO LET PLYMOUTH HOLD A MARKET...

(9)

CELT
500 BC

ROMAN
AD 43-410

ANGLO-
SAXON
AD 450-
1066

VIKING
AD 865-
1066

MEDIEVAL
TIMES
1066-
1485

A Fishy Story

The smell of fish masks the stench of the horse manure and other rubbish in the streets as a boat with a bulging catch is unloaded at the quayside. It's a busy scene although it's still only 6 o'clock. The ship builders and sail and rope makers are working hard. Noisy seagulls circle over the heads of the fishermen as they land their wriggling booty. Some of the local fishermen have sailed as far as Newfoundland on the other side of the Atlantic, to reap their fishy harvests. Some of the hardiest sailors are from around here!

Drake, the Pirate!

Oh goodie, which Spanish ship can I raid next?

In the 16th century, England's European neighbours were sailing to the New World (the Americas, Africa and the West Indies) in search of riches. Francis Drake was a sea captain and privateer born in Tavistock, Devon, in 1540. He plundered Spanish treasure ships wherever he could find them, making a fortune for his queen (Elizabeth I) and country – and for himself. But many people, especially the Spanish, thought he was no better than a pirate! Drake had upset the Spanish many times and, with so many of the townsmen away at sea at any one time, the people of Plymouth lived in constant fear of attack. There were even fines for those who didn't take their turn at keeping watch. Meanwhile, the queen announced that Wednesdays, Fridays and Saturdays would be meatless days, increasing demand for fish. Plymouth prospered, and almost doubled in size under her rule!

You will eat fish and you will like it!

Spanish Armada

In 1588, the people of Plymouth's fears were realised, when King Philip II of Spain launched an attack to overthrow Queen Elizabeth. A huge fleet of ships, known as the Spanish Armada, set sail for Plymouth. Elizabeth ordered a counter-attack, led by Drake. His fleet chased the Spaniards out to sea and launched flaming 'fire ships' into the enemy fleet. A month after setting sail, the Armada was defeated, with a little help from the stormy weather.

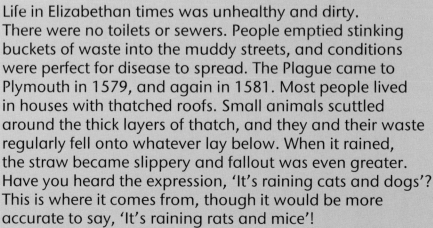

This is an engraving showing the defeat of the Spanish Armada on 30 May 1588.

According to legend, Drake was playing bowls on the Hoe when he heard the Armada was coming. "We have time to finish this game, and beat the Spaniards too!" he boldly said.

The Merchant's House is Plymouth's best surviving example of a Tudor home. What a lot of windows to clean!

Tudor Life

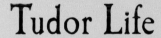

Life in Elizabethan times was unhealthy and dirty. There were no toilets or sewers. People emptied stinking buckets of waste into the muddy streets, and conditions were perfect for disease to spread. The Plague came to Plymouth in 1579, and again in 1581. Most people lived in houses with thatched roofs. Small animals scuttled around the thick layers of thatch, and they and their waste regularly fell onto whatever lay below. When it rained, the straw became slippery and fallout was even greater. Have you heard the expression, 'It's raining cats and dogs'? This is where it comes from, though it would be more accurate to say, 'It's raining rats and mice'!

There were several wells in the town — many of them recalled in street names today: Finewell, Buckwell, Westwell, Holywell, Ladywell. You'd go to 'fine well' for drinking water — water from 'buck well' was fit only for washing, or bucking, clothes.

Young William Martyn is by far the luckiest in his family. Why? Because he's the only one who goes to school; so he's also the only one who can read and write. Three long years ago, his father, Thomas, sailed off with Francis Drake on his 'great voyage'. His Uncle Nicholas went, too. Over a year ago they heard that Drake had been seen on the Pacific Coast of the Americas, but that was the only news – until yesterday!

I can't wait to hear the stories Father has to tell!

On completion of their epic three-year journey in 1580, Drake and his crew became the first Englishmen to sail around the world. Drake captured a huge amount of treasure, mainly from Spanish ships. Queen Elizabeth knighted him Sir Francis Drake in 1581 for his enormous contribution to the country's wealth. Drake also paid all his men well – the highest ranks were able to buy new houses.

September 1580

Drake has returned! Who can believe it? He refused to land at first, until he had been convinced that Queen Elizabeth was still alive – and still queen. Drake's wife, Mary, went out to meet the ship with the Mayor but, on learning there was plague in town, Drake decided to take his treasure ship straight up to the queen in London. Then a small crew of men was spotted rowing ashore. Father was among them! My little brothers didn't recognise him – they were so young when he went away – but I did.

It's been hard for Mother looking after the family since Father left with Drake on his grand voyage. We've had little money. I feel like I have lived off bread and disgusting ale although the ale is safer to drink than the water. It has been hard to sleep well. Our house has been overrun with those dratted bugs dropping off the thatch onto our bed. Mother was going to put a canopy up, but she has been so busy with her job – combing hemp for rope. As we live along the rope walk, it's been easy to sell. I know things will be better now with Father back.

TUDOR 1485-1603
STUART 1603-1714
GEORGIAN 1714-1837
VICTORIAN 1837-1901
MODERN TIMES 1902-NOW

A New Street

Plymouth's New Street is still there today, but it was 'new' in Queen Elizabeth's time – 450 years ago! Greyfriar's Monastery originally stood on the land, but this had been shut down and sold off by Queen Elizabeth's father, Henry VIII. Henry had decided to make himself (instead of the Pope) head of the English church. Having done that, he closed down all the monasteries in the country and pocketed the proceeds.

John Sparke – a Devon merchant and later Mayor of Plymouth – built a number of houses on the site of the old monastery. They were typical of the time, but with more glass windows than anyone had seen before. The windows weren't just to allow daylight in ... they also kept bad smells out! Many of these houses were snapped up by wealthy sea farers.

SPOT THIS!

If you go to the Elizabethan House look out for a baby's cot. People say it rocks by itself! Spooky or what?

Elizabethan House

See how people lived in the Elizabethan House. How are our houses different?

How do we know?

There are many buildings still standing from Tudor times that tell us what life was like in Plymouth. A few of the old merchants' and sea captains' houses still stand on the Barbican (the name means 'fortress by the water') and two of them are even open to the public. Both are built mainly of wood, most likely made from the timbers of old ships. Once a ship had served its time at sea it would be sold and broken up. Because its timbers were old, and no longer likely to shrink or bend, they made good building material. The staircase of a new house was often built around the mast of an old ship, like the one in the Elizabethan House on New Street. In fact, the Barbican has over 200 historic buildings, and the largest area of cobbled streets anywhere in England!

CELT
500 BC

ROMAN
AD 43-410

ANGLO-
SAXON
AD 450-
1066

VIKING
AD 865-
1066

MEDIEVA
TIMES
1066-
1485

Siege!

The winter of 1643 is bitterly cold, and Plymouth is under siege. The King's Royalist troops have cut off food supplies and diverted the fresh water supply away from the town. The 10,000 freezing and hungry locals have to share what little food and water they have with thousands of Roundhead troops who are stationed in the forts surrounding the town.

Gruel, gruel and more gruel...

I know, it's really gruelling!

Plymouth sided with us Roundheads. The town was besieged by Royalists for four years but we fought them off!

Civil War

In 1642, the English Civil War broke out. Many people did not like the way the king ruled or the way he treated people who criticized him. For many years people had also argued about religion. Some people, such as the Pilgrim Fathers, felt that they needed to leave the country so they could worship in the way they wanted.

Over the next four years, a series of bloody battles was fought between the Royalists (supporters of King Charles I) and the Roundheads (supporters of Parliament).

Traitors' Tales

In November 1643, local resident Mr Carkeet was arrested for scheming to blow up Maudlyn Fort (on what is now North Hill), in order to let the Royalists into Plymouth. He was desperate – all of the town were – with scarcely any food and the Plague spreading.

A few days later, two more local traitors, lawyer Moses Collins and wine merchant Henry Pike, secretly advised Royalist troops how best to attack the town. In the early hours of Sunday morning, Collins and Pike led the king's men across the freezing waters of Lipson Creek. The fort at Laira Point was taken completely by surprise. Royalist horsemen rode to within yards of the town, but the Roundheads chased them back towards the creek. Many Royalist men were shot or drowned in the icy waters.

...1620 MAYFLOWER SETS SAIL FOR AMERICA...

TUDOR
1485-1603

STUART
1603-1714

GEORGIAN
1714-1837

VICTORIAN
1837-1901

MODERN TIMES
1902-NOW

Royalists Remember

Plymouth was the only town in England that managed to withstand a Royalist siege, and the Royalists never forgot it. Leader of the Roundheads, Oliver Cromwell, had King Charles I tried and executed in 1649 for treason. Cromwell then ruled England as Lord Protector for a short time. He helped to establish Plymouth as an important port, building a Victualling Yard (to supply the navy with food and drink) just beyond the Barbican.

Soon after Cromwell died, however, Charles I's son (also called Charles) won back the throne. Charles II wasted no time in building a massive stone fort in Plymouth. The fort, named the Royal Citadel, was designed partly to help defend the town, but also – it was said – so the king could be sure that the people of Plymouth would never again be in a position to oppose the Royal cause.

All Aboard!

My name is William Brewster. I'm travelling on the Mayflower with my wife, Mary, and sons, Love and Wrestling.

In 1620, the *Mayflower* embarked on her famous voyage. The ship left Plymouth, near the site of the Mayflower Steps, carrying 102 pilgrims plus crew. The passengers, known as the Pilgrim Fathers, wanted to begin a new life where they could freely practise their religion. The ship was destined for the Hudson River, near present-day New York City, but it went off course and settled in Cape Cod Bay, Plymouth, Massachusetts, in the United States.

The journey took 66 days, and two passengers died on the way. The *Mayflower* voyage was seen as an important event in the founding of America. It is why many Americans still visit the Mayflower Steps today, some of them trying to trace their ancestors who set sail nearly 400 years ago.

This illustration of a stained glass window shows King Charles I talking to his Royalist troops on the battlefield. Supporters of Charles I, and later his son, fought in many fierce battles between 1642 and 1651.

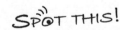

SPOT THIS!

This stone carving of the Mayflower ship can be found in the Elizabethan garden off Southside Street.

CELT
500 BC

ROMAN
AD 43-410

ANGLO-
SAXON
AD 450-
1066

VIKING
AD 865-
1066

MEDIEVAL
TIMES
1066-
1485

His Majesty's Dockyard

The early morning wake-up call stirs the men from their slumbers. Their hammocks didn't sway so much last night – the grey waters of the Hamoaze were still and calm. They slip waistcoats, jackets and sturdy leggings on over their nightshirts before lining up for a plate of bread and cheese. After breakfast, the men drop down over the side of the ship to be rowed to the shore to work in His Majesty's new dockyard. Most of the workers are shipwrights, but some are general labourers.

Look out below!

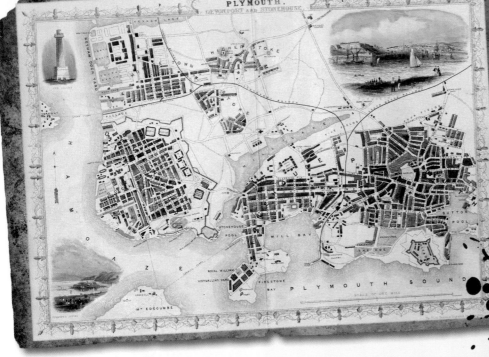

This map dating from 1860 shows the dockyard to the east of Plymouth. There was a lot of work for men in the ropeyard and the sawpits.

Much of England was once covered in trees, but the Navy turned most of them into wooden warships!

The New Dock

With Plymouth's remarkable sea-going history it is easy to see why, in 1690, King William III chose the Hamoaze – just along the coast from the town – as the site for an important new dockyard. By 1698 the dock had taken shape, and it soon made its mark on Plymouth.

Hundreds of men arrived, eager for work, but the Hamoaze didn't have room for them all! Old warships, stripped of their masts and sails, were used as lodgings. Workers from Plymouth had a long walk to get there – it took over an hour, and they were often robbed on their way home!

...1690 WORK STARTS ON DOCKYARD, COMMISSIONED BY WILLIAM III...

Wooden warships in the water beside the dockyard in 1735. Imagine what people back then would say if they saw the warships that are now docked in Plymouth!

The First Ships

The first two boats built in the yard were small — 73-ton vessels, with four guns each. It wasn't until 1696 that the first substantial ship, called the *Looe*, was built entirely at the new dockyard. Devastatingly, however, less than a year later, news filtered back that this 400-ton warship had struck a rock near Baltimore in North America and sunk. The ship was lost but, happily, the entire crew were saved.

The waters around Great Britain were no safer. In 1703, the Great Storm sank seven warships along one 6-kilometre stretch of the Kent coastline. Over 1,500 men went down with the ships that night — roughly a fifth of the Navy's manpower at the time. Only the ship-building industry benefited.

All this boat building has brought on a thirst.

I'll drink to that!

...1696 WARSHIP THE *LOOE* IS BUILT...1703 GREAT STORM RAGES...

17

A Bright Idea

In less than 100 years, the dockyard at the Hamoaze had grown bigger than Plymouth itself. As it grew more important, so did all the approaches to it – across land, river and particularly by sea.

The English and French navies – and countless merchant traders – had lost ships on the Eddystone Reef, 22 kilometres off the Plymouth coast. Eccentric merchant and engineer Henry Winstanley was determined to find a solution to the problem. He designed and built a fantastic wooden lighthouse, which he believed could withstand any storm...

SPOT THIS!

John Smeaton built the third lighthouse on the Eddystone Reef in 1759. A paving stone monument to it can be seen in the town. Can you spot the engraved plaques and find out more about the tower's history?

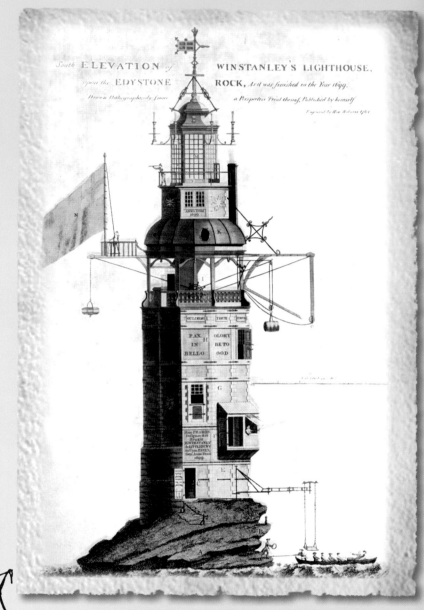

Winstanley's Eddystone Lighthouse was the first to be built on a rock in the open ocean. The light was lit on 14 November 1698 and, with running repairs and improvements by Winstanley, the lighthouse survived several harsh winters.

Great Storm

On 28 November 1703, the greatest storm ever witnessed raged across the south of England. Ships were wrecked and blown off course, and buildings were razed to the ground. Over 8,000 lives were lost – most of them men drowned at sea.

The storms blew inland, too. In London, a whole street of houses was flattened. In Plymouth, two boys were watching the storm from behind the old fish house on the Barbican. They were swept away on a huge wave – never to be seen again.

Winstanley was determined to prove that his lighthouse could withstand any weather the English Channel could throw at it. On the night of 28 November 1703, he decided to stay in the lighthouse to do repairs. This is an imaginary report based on a real-life event, told by Brian, the lighthouse keeper's son, who is 10 years old.

It's a fine, strong lighthouse, but this is a terrible storm!

Father didn't sleep at the lighthouse last night. It was his turn to keep the lamps alight, but he's taken to his bed with a fever. A terrible storm has been raging for days. The waves have been as tall as houses! The wind has been howling through the city but people are staying in their homes.

I would love to meet Mr Winstanley – the clever gentleman who built the tower. There had been a lull in the storm and even though people said the storm was going to get much worse, Mr Winstanley still went out with a group of workmen to make repairs. No men have been lost in the waters around Plymouth since his fine lighthouse was lit five years ago, and no ships have run aground on the dangerous rocks. Winstanley wanted to prove the strength of his creation to the whole world. What a brave fellow! I fell asleep listening to the wind screaming and the waves crashing. When I woke in the morning, the world seemed quiet and eerie. Then I heard the news. The lighthouse was gone! It had completely vanished from the rocks! How lucky Father is. I feel sad for Mr Winstanley and the brave lighthouse keepers, but we will always remember them.

How do we know?

It was widely reported that Henry Winstanley wanted to prove the strength of his lighthouse by staying on it during a terrible storm.

Author Daniel Defoe gives a graphic account of the Great Storm in his collection of eyewitness accounts called 'The Storm', published the following year, 1704.

Hoorah for Devonport!

> I now declare Plymouth Dock is renamed Devonport!

There are flags fluttering all over town! Mr Rodd, the Town Clerk, has been rushing through the streets, stopping every now and then to announce the message sent from London by Mr Robert Peel (the Home Secretary). It states that His Majesty, King George IV, agrees to the town's petition to change the name from Plymouth Dock to Devonport. Here and there a trumpet sounds, and everyone is making merry – the taverns are doing an excellent trade!

The Theatre Royal and Royal Hotel were the grandest buildings in the town.

Theatre Royal

Architect Mr Foulston came to Plymouth in 1810 to design the Theatre Royal. Foulston insisted the theatre was built on the edge of town, as he realised it would need to attract people from neighbouring areas to survive. He also created a new road to make it easier for people to get there – it was called Union Street. Despite this, the Theatre Royal struggled to make a profit for many years.

It was pulled down four years before the Blitz that destroyed the adjoining Royal Hotel.

Celebratory Column

In 1822 a new Town Hall, also designed by Mr Foulston, was completed in Devonport. Just two years later, Foulston drew up plans for a column – celebrating the town's change of name – to be erected alongside the new Town Hall. The Town Hall was modelled on the Parthenon – an ancient Greek temple – and the column was in the Roman style.

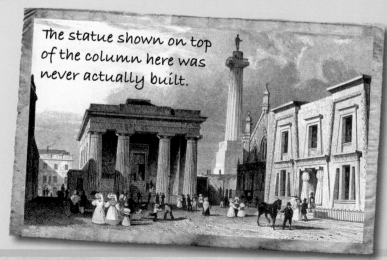

The statue shown on top of the column here was never actually built.

UDOR 1485-1603	STUART 1603-1714	GEORGIAN 1714-1837	VICTORIAN 1837-1901	MODERN TIMES 1902-NOW

John Foulston was 38 years old, and had a successful architectural practice in London, when he left to begin a new life in the South West of England. This is an imaginary account based on the real-life event of his arrival in Plymouth in 1810.

John Foulston died in 1841, and is buried in St Andrew's cemetery in Plymouth.

It was a fine spring day when I came to the Three Towns of Plymouth, Devonport and Stonehouse. As my carriage rounded a bend in the road, I caught a captivating glimpse of the ocean sparkling blue and green in the distance.

My first meeting was with the Mayor, Mr Lockyer, to claim my 50 guinea prize for winning his competition to design the town's new theatre and hotel. I simply could not wait to begin work on the buildings. I had so many grand and exciting ideas! I planned to design the theatre to look like a great Roman temple, with towering pillars at the entrance and a huge auditorium. The hotel would be just as spectacular, with a special room for storing ice.

I longed to create buildings all across the Three Towns and beyond in exotic Roman, Greek and Egyptian styles. All I hoped was that my beautiful buildings would stand the test of time. I wanted to be remembered for many years to come.

How do we know?

Although many of John Foulston's buildings were destroyed by bombs during the Second World War, some are still standing today. Despite a number of fires in the late 1800s, the Theatre Royal was still in use until 1937, when it was finally demolished to make way for a modern cinema.

SP☺T THIS!

Designed by Foulston and originally called Oddfellows Hall, this Egyptian-style building is now the Ker Street Social Club. Can you spot it?

The First Train

Millbay Station was a crowded blaze of colour. Banners and bunting danced in the spring breeze as the music of the Royal Marine Band signalled the arrival of Plymouth's very first 'Iron Horse'. The Industrial Revolution had come to Plymouth! All over Britain, new industries and mass production were changing people's lives, as they journeyed from the countryside to find work and homes in the growing towns and cities. The splendid new network of railways that stretched up and down the country helped to make those journeys possible.

Millbay Railway Station first opened in 1849. Trains had to stop at a ticket platform for tickets to be collected before going on to the main station.

Not So Quicksilver

For most people, the arrival of the first train into Millbay Station was something to celebrate. The fastest horse-drawn coach was the Quicksilver, which took four hours to reach Exeter, and a horrifying 20 hours to reach London. Now Exeter was less than two hours away, and London less than six!

The new train made longer journeys possible for everyone. Comfortable first-class travel was beyond most people's budget, but second-class carriages were reasonably priced – they had no windows, but at least they had a roof. Third class was the cheapest option, but you'd be travelling in open trucks at 30 km per hour!

Thank goodness I'm travelling second-class. It's started to rain!

Brunel's Bridge

The Royal Albert Bridge, which links Devon with Cornwall over the River Tamar, was designed by Isambard Kingdom Brunel, and opened in 1859. One hundred and fifty years later, the bridge is still in everyday use, carrying the only railway route that runs deep into the heart of Cornwall.

Guests from Cornwall were late for the opening ceremony as their train broke down!

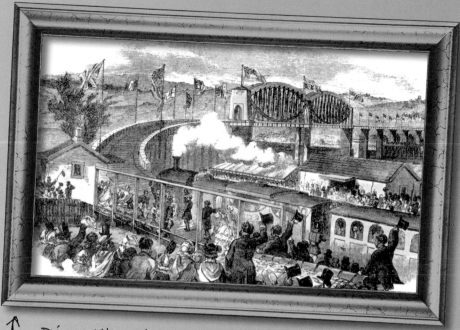

Prince Albert himself performed the opening ceremony on 2 May 1859, but Brunel was ill and unable to attend.

What Effect Did It Have?

The railway made some people rich, but many railway labourers were forced to work long hours for poor wages. Only the wealthiest travellers could afford to stay in the Duke of Cornwall Hotel that opened opposite the station in 1865.

Plymouth grew spectacularly in the 1800s. In 1800, it had a population of around 16,000. It was a little smaller than Exeter and a lot smaller than the next-door town of Devonport. However, by the time Queen Victoria died in 1901, Plymouth had a population of 107,000. It was twice the size of Exeter and much bigger than Devonport, thanks, in large part, to the railway.

My name, I. K. Brunel, appears in large metal letters on both ends of the bridge.

How do we know?

Plenty of newspaper reports survive from this time, and census returns tell us how many local people had jobs connected to the railway. There are also advertisements for the coaches and time tables for the train services.

All that remains of the old station are a couple of granite pillars that once stood at its entrance. Next time you go to The Pavilions, see if you can spot them. The Duke of Cornwall Hotel is still there today.

...1859 ISAMBARD KINGDOM BRUNEL DIES...

CELT
500 BC

ROMAN
AD 43-410

ANGLO-
SAXON
AD 450-
1066

VIKING
AD 865-
1066

MEDIEVAL
TIMES
1066-
1485

Between the Wars

There is so much to see in the city! Engines purr and horns toot loudly. Some people say that every family will own a car in the future – can you imagine it?! There are even special places to cross the road so it's safe. Tall black and white poles with a big yellow ball on the top. They look funny but their name is even funnier – Belisha Beacons! Whatever next!

Thank you for waiting!

Progress

The 1920s and 1930s were exciting decades for Plymouth. In 1928 it became a city; Plymouth Argyle Football and Plymouth Albion Rugby clubs were both doing well; and, with no TV, people were flocking to the cinema. In November 1930, two new venues – the Regent and the Gaumont – opened. The Regent was then one of the biggest cinemas in Europe.

With more transport on the road than ever before, Devonport MP, Leslie Hore Belisha (who was also the government's Minister for Transport), introduced the driving test, traffic lights and the 'Belisha' beacons you can still find next to all zebra crossings.

Electricity in the Home

Life at home was becoming more comfortable between the First and Second World Wars. In 1926, the Central Electricity Generating Board was established and more and more Plymouth houses were supplied with electricity. Electricity meant people didn't have to rely on gas lights, oil lamps or candles. And, if you could afford it, you could buy fantastic luxury items, such as electric irons, kettles and vacuum cleaners. You didn't need mains electricity to operate a 'wireless', though. Instead you'd use a big, heavy battery, called an accumulator. It was like a small car battery. It was often the children's job to carry it down to the local garage for recharging.

I don't know whether to go to the cinema or stay at home and watch my new electric kettle boil!

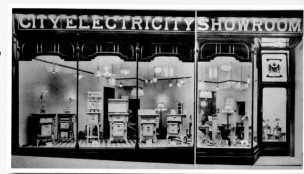

The showroom had electrical goods people could hire and it also held cookery demonstrations.

Blitz

Plymouth was very badly damaged during the Second World War. Between 1939 and 1945, the German Luftwaffe (air force) attacked Plymouth and other targets in Britain regularly and often successfully. The very first attack on Plymouth came in June 1940, just after France had fallen to the Germans. Then in March and April 1941, over a period of seven nights, Plymouth suffered its worst air raids. These were referred to as 'the Blitz'. Altogether, Plymouth suffered 59 bombing raids and the air-raid sirens sounded over 600 times.

That was the worst raid yet. We're lucky we got under cover in time.

This photograph shows the damage to Drake Circus after the Blitz. A fireman is still hosing a building the day after the bombs were dropped.

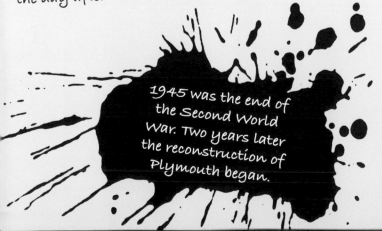

1945 was the end of the Second World War. Two years later the reconstruction of Plymouth began.

A Plan for Plymouth

Even before the war had ended in 1945, it was decided that Plymouth could not be rebuilt to how it was before in 1939. The former traffic congestion and narrow streets were no longer practical. On 1 September 1941, the City Council decided that a new plan was needed for Plymouth.

Lord Astor was Lord Mayor and he persuaded the famous town planner Professor Abercrombie to help the City Engineer, James Paton Watson, redesign the city. They produced their plan in 1943, two years after the Blitz. In order to realise their vision for Plymouth they would need to clear the whole of the city centre, including buildings that were still standing. In clearing over 28 hectares of land they pulled down a lot of buildings that had survived the war so they could begin Plymouth's transformation.

Cyril is at Hyde Park Junior School. His dad's away in the Navy, and he hasn't seen him for over two years. His brother George has just gone off to Portsmouth as a naval cadet. His mother is struggling to make ends meet. The war started a year and a half ago and already there have been 275 bomb alerts, and 30 actual attacks. But then came two really heavy raids on the nights of 20 and 21 March 1941...

I've got used to carrying my gas mask around.

Dear George   22 March 1941

Great news! Last night incendiaries hit our school and once the top floor caught fire, it burned out completely. So school is closed! Luckily the sirens wailed in good time, and we got to the shelter before we heard German Heinkel bombers throbbing and droning across the city. I used to think the bombings were exciting, but now it's just frightening. I feel sorry for people who live in the centre of town. At least we're high up here in Hermitage Road and a little too far away from the shopping centre and the dockyard for the bombers to be interested.

Mum wanted me to stay in today, but she had to go and help out at Freedom Fields hospital. So I sneaked into town. I hardly recognised the place! There was dirt and dust and the smell of smoke everywhere. Whole streets were cordoned off. I saw one family staring at a hole in the ground where their home used to be. They'd been in a shelter all night - in their nightclothes - and now everything they owned had been burned to a cinder.

There were fire engines in town from all over Devon. But only the Plymouth Fire Brigade could connect their hoses to the water supply, so they ended up getting hardly any help at all.

Later, I bumped into Jim from school. He'd been on the Hoe, where the pier had been bombed. The pinball machines at the entrance were wrecked and pennies had spilled out of them all over the rocks. His pockets were bulging!

As we walked home I swapped a couple of pieces of shrapnel I'd found on North Hill for some of his loot, and we had great fun choosing chocolate and liquorice strips in the tuck shop next to school. We were having a real laugh, but then, as we were standing on the corner talking, Jim noticed something on the pavement and picked it up. It was somebody's finger!

Mum's worried about Dad. We haven't had a letter in weeks now. She's worried about you too.

Write soon,
Cyril

MODERN TIMES 1902-NOW

The Recovery of Plymouth

If it hadn't been for the war, Plymouth's population would have got smaller – the war brought jobs that meant people could stay in the area. In the 1940s and 1950s, spacious new estates were built around the city to house people whose homes had been destroyed during the war.

Plymouth Guildhall was one of the lucky pre-war buildings to escape the 'Plan for Plymouth'. Although it survived the Blitz, the inside was destroyed by fire during the night of the 21/22 March 1941. The Council felt the foundations were solid enough to rebuild, and so work began in 1953 to restore it.

Derry's Clock also still stands in its original place. Although it is now surrounded by modern buildings, the people of Plymouth have protested against plans to move it to a more prominent position in the town.

When Derry's Clock was built in the 1860s, it was in the very centre of the city.

Plymouth has more post-war listed buildings than anywhere in England outside London.

SPOT THIS!

Have you looked up to see the stone statues around the Guildhall?

How do we know?

We have plenty of film, photographs and first-hand accounts – and there are still people around today who can remember what it was like living in Plymouth during the Blitz. You can also see gas masks and air-raid shelters, which show how people tried to keep themselves safe.

Plymouth has changed drastically since the war, but there are still some old buildings around – especially in the Barbican. Both the Regent and the Gaumont cinemas survived the Second World War. The Gaumont building has been closed for many years, but it still stands in Union Street, opposite the Pavilions pool.

...1947 RECONSTRUCTION OF PLYMOUTH BEGINS...

Plymouth Today and Tomorrow...

We know about the history of Plymouth from the things people have left behind. Buildings, written records and artefacts are some of the important things which help us to understand the town's past. But what will we leave behind for our children and our children's children to discover?

Plymouth is the wettest city in England according to the Met office!

Smeaton's Tower is one of the most recognised landmarks on the Hoe and open to the public. Will it stand the test of time and still be a landmark in 100 years' time?

I want to take a photo from the top of Smeaton's Tower.

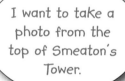

Plymouth Barbican has witnessed some historical moments. It's where Drake set sail and where the Pilgrim Fathers set off to begin their new lives in America. Will the Barbican see more historic events?

SPOT THIS!

Does this statue of a man doing a handstand look familiar? Next time you're out shopping at Drake Circus – look up!

...1935 PLYMOUTH'S FIRST LORD MAYOR APPOINTED...

The Tamar Bridge, located above the Hamoaze and next to Brunel's bridge, is still used today. It has been widened and strengthened, but will it be able to cope with the increasing traffic in the future?

How will they know?

We only have to click onto the Internet to find proof of how we live our lives. We upload pictures, keep blogs and send emails. Will the Internet act as a museum in the future? Should we still keep artefacts for future generations to see and touch? How much of today's Plymouth will still exist in 10, 100 or 1,000 years' time?

The Guildhall managed to survive the Blitz. Will it be standing in your grandchildren's lifetime and what will the building be used for?

Drake Circus Shopping Centre has transformed throughout the years. In the 1970s a bigger Drake Circus Shopping Centre replaced the pre-war building. Then in 2003 it was pulled down to make way for the shopping centre we see today. How long will the new shopping centre last?

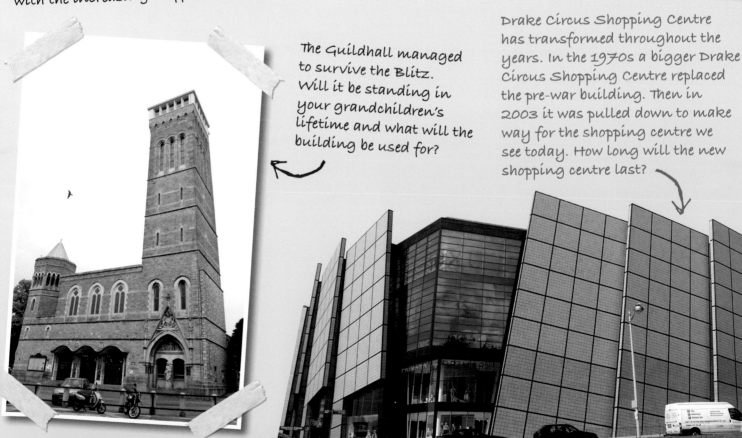

Glossary

AD – a short way of writing the Latin words anno Domini, which mean 'in the year of our Lord', i.e. after the birth of Christ.

Air raid – during the Second World War enemy planes dropped bombs on Britain. This was called an air raid. To warn people to hide, air-raid sirens wailed out all over the city.

Artefact – another word for an object, often an archaeological one.

BC – a short way of writing 'before the birth of Christ'.

Breakwater – a wall built out into the sea to protect a harbour from waves.

Bronze Age – a period in history from about 2000 to 500 BC during which weapons and tools were made from bronze.

Domesday Book – William the Conqueror sent his men all over England to check how much land and wealth was in the kingdom, and who owned it. The results of this survey were written in a book called the Domesday Book, which survives to this day.

Gargoyle – a spout carved in the form of an ugly face or figure sticking out from a gutter to carry rainwater clear of the wall.

Guinea – an old British gold coin worth 21 shillings (£1.05).

Incendiaries – bombs designed to start fires, used during the Second World War.

Industrial Revolution – a period from the 18th to the 19th century when big changes in agriculture, manufacturing, mining and transport occurred, beginning with the invention of steam-powered machines.

Isthmus – a narrow strip of land joining two large areas of land.

Motte – a mound on which a castle was built.

Pagan – someone who believes in more than one god.

Pilgrim – a person who goes on a journey, sometimes to a sacred place.

Priory – a religious house such as an abbey or monastery.

Quayside – the area near a quay (a wharf).

Ration book – during the Second World War, certain food was scarce and had to be rationed. Your Ration Book showed how much of this food you could have every week. Once you'd used it up, you wouldn't get any more until the next week.

Roundhead – anyone who fought on the side of Parliament against Charles I in the English Civil War.

Royalist – anyone who fought on the side of King Charles I in the English Civil War.

Shipwright – someone who builds or repairs ships.

Shrapnel – fragments that break off from bombs or bullets.

Siege – when people try to capture a place by surrounding or blockading it.

Stannary – a tin mine.

Traitor – someone who is guilty of treason.

Treason – to be disloyal to the king or queen.

Victualling yard – an area where food and drink is stored ready to be supplied to the navy.

Index

Acknowledgements

The author and publishers would like to thank Chris Robinson for his generous help.

The publishers would like to thank the following people and organizations
for their permission to reproduce material on the following pages:

p11: The Art Archive/Alamy; p12: Mary Evans Picture Library; p15: www.chrisrobinson.co.uk,
Copyright Highton-Ridley.co.uk, 2008; p16: Reproduced with the permission of the Plymouth and West Devon Record
Office. Reference 2404/13; p17: www.chrisrobinson.co.uk; p18: www.chrisrobinson.co.uk;
p20: www.chrisrobinson.co.uk; p22: www.chrisrobinson.co.uk; p23: www.chrisrobinson.co.uk;
p24: www.chrisrobinson.co.uk; p25: www.chrisrobinson.co.uk

All other images copyright of Hometown World

Written by Chris Robinson
Educational consultant: Neil Thompson
Local history consultant: Anne Morgan
Designed by Stephen Prosser

Illustrated by Leo Brown, Kate Davies, Dynamo Ltd, Peter Kent, Kevin Kimber,
John MacGregor, Victor Mclindon, Leighton Noyes, Tim Sutcliffe
Additional photographs by Alex Long

First published by HOMETOWN WORLD in 2010
Hometown World Ltd
7 Northumberland Buildings
Bath BA1 2JB

www.hometownworld.co.uk

ISBN 978-1-84993-008-6

Your past
Your now
Your future

Your history4ever

Mmm... Still love chocolate pudding!

My next one's going to have 2 wheels!

Trophy for the trendiest glasses?

I love you too!